D0984578

~ MYTHOLOGY ~

CELTIC MYTHOLOGY

Catherine Bernard

Enslow Publishers, Inc.

40 Industrial Road   PO Box 38
Box 398   Aldershot
Berkeley Heights, NJ 07922   Hants GU12 6BP
USA   UK

http://www.enslow.com

For the Cunningham, Daley, and Collins clans

Enslow Publishers, Inc., wishes to thank Professor Daniel Melia of the University of California Celtic Studies Program for his invaluable assistance with the pronunciation guide.

Library of Congress Cataloging-in-Publication Data

Bernard, Catherine.
    Celtic mythology / Catherine Bernard.
        p. cm.
    Summary: Introduces the Celts and their mythology, relating seven tales with their roots primarily in Ireland and Wales and placing each in historical and cultural context.
    Includes bibliographical references and index.
    ISBN 0-7660-2204-8
    1. Mythology, Celtic—Juvenile literature.   [1. Mythology, Celtic.]   I. Title.
    BL900.B47 2003
    398.2'089'916—dc21

                          2002152978

Printed in the United States of America

10 9 8 7 6 5 4 3 2 1

Cover and illustrations by William Sauts Bock

Contents

CELTIC NAMES AND PLACES

Pronouncing Irish Words

- When pronouncing Irish words, stress usually falls heavily on the first syllable. Vowels in unaccented syllables, particularly final syllables, are schwas—the neutral vowel sound found, for instance, in the first syllable of "pajamas" or the "a" in "about," and phonetically represented here as "uh."
- "Ch" represents the sound found in Scots "loch" or German "ach."
- "Gh" represents a soft, guttural sound.
- There are two "th" sounds: one as in "thin" (represented here as "th") and one as in "this" (represented here as "th").
- "B" and "m," when not the first letter in a word, are, roughly, like an English "v."
- "S," when preceded or followed by an "i" or "e," is like the English "sh."

Pronouncing Welsh Words

- Stress in Welsh is usually on the next-to-last (penultimate) syllable of a word, as in Latin. Welsh has the same "th" contrast between unvoiced ("th") and voiced ("th") forms as do Irish and English.
- "Ch" represents the sound found in Scots "loch" or German "ach."
- "Gh" is a soft guttural sound.
- Sounds that do not occur in English include unvoiced "l," spelled "ll" and pronounced like "tl" said quickly. (To make this sound in the Welsh fashion, place one side of the tongue lightly between the upper and lower teeth on one side of the mouth and blow gently.)
- "Rh" is approximated by pronouncing it as if written "hr"; plain Welsh "r" is lightly trilled with the tip of the tongue.
- As a vowel, "w" is pronounced "oo" if long and "u" if short. When a consonant, "w" is pronounced as in English.
- "U," when short, is like the "i" in "pill", when long, like "ee" as in "feed."
- "Y" has three sounds, depending on its length and whether it is in a final syllable: "ee" as in "feed," "i" as in "pin," and "uh" as in "but."
- A single "f" is pronounced as "v."

The suggested pronunciations are very approximate.

Aife (EE-fuh or AYE-fuh)—Scathach's enemy, who is defeated by Cúchulainn.

Amargin (AV-ar-ghin)—Druid who helps the Milesians defeat the Tuatha Dé Danaan.

Annwn (AH-noon)—The Underworld.

Aranrhod (ah-RAN-rhode)—Mother of Lleu Llaw Gyffes.

Arawn (AH-raun)—Lord of the Underworld, who switches places for one year with Pwyll.

Balor (BAH-lohr)—Greatest and most evil of Fomori kings; he was nicknamed "of the Evil Eye."

Banba (BAN-buh)—Danaan queen who asks the Milesians to name the island after her, should they conquer Ireland.

Bedwyr (BED-weer)—Knight in Arthur's court whose special skill is speed with his sword.

Blodeuwedd (BLOW-DYE-we<u>th</u>)—Woman created out of flowers by Math and Gwydion so that Lleu Llaw Gyffes might have a wife.

Bres (BRESS)—Chosen king of the Tuatha dé Danaan after Nuada loses his hand; he is overthrown once Nuada is healed and declares war on the Tuatha Dé Danaan.

Cian (KEY-ann)—Lugh's Danaan father.

Conchobar (KON-cho-var)—King of Ulster and foster father to Cúchulainn in the Red Branch Cycle of myths.

Cúchulainn (KOO-CHUHL-uhn)—Hero of the myths of the Red Branch Cycle.

Culhwch (KILL-hookh)—Hero of the best-known Welsh tale concerning King Arthur and his knights.

Dagda (DAHG-<u>th</u>ah)—Father of the gods; he was Cúchulainn's maternal grandfather.

Danu (DAN-oo)—Mother of the gods; the Tuatha Dé Danaan are named after her.

Dian Cécht (DEE-uhn KAYCHT)—God of medicine who makes Nuada a silver hand.

Dyfed (DUH-ved)—Region in southern Wales ruled by Pwyll.

Elatha (ELL-uh-thuh)—King of the Fomori and Bres's father.

Emer (AY-ver)—Cúchulainn's wife.

Eochaid (YOCH-ee or YOCH-i<u>th</u>)—Firbolg king who is killed in the battle with the Tuatha Dé Danaan.

Eriu (AY-ryoo)—Danaan queen who asks the Milesians to name the island after her, should they conquer Ireland.

Ethne (ETH-nuh)—Lugh's mother.

Fenians (FEE-nee-ans)—Band of warriors who followed Finn mac Cumaill.

Finn mac Cumaill (FIN mak KOOL or FIN mak KOOVAL)—Main hero of the myths of the Fenian Cycle.

Firbolg (FEER-bowl-uhg)—Misshapen and stupid race that battles the Tuatha Dé Danaan.

Fomori (foe-MORE-ee)—Strange beings, sometimes depicted as giants, who inhabit Ireland.

Fotla (FODE-luh)—Danaan queen who asks the Milesians to name the island after her, should they conquer Ireland.

Goibniu (GOYV-nee-oo)—Danaan smith god who instantly crafts new spears for his people during their battle with the Firbolgs.

Gronw Pebyr (GRON-oo PEB-eer)—Blodeuwedd's lover, who plots with her to kill Lleu Llaw Gyffes.

Gwalchmei (GWALCH-may)—Knight

in Arthur's court who could leave no adventure unexplored.

Gwawl (GWOWL)—Man to whom Rhiannon had been promised.

Gwrhyr (GOOR-heer)—Knight in Arthur's court who is able to speak the language of any man or animal.

Gwydion (GWID-ee-on)—Welsh god of illusion and poetry; Lleu Llaw Gyffes's adoptive father.

Hafgan (HAHV-gahn)—Arawn's rival in the Underworld. Pwyll agrees to fight him in Arawn's place.

Lleu Llaw Gyffes (LLAY-oo LLAU-oo GUFF-ess)—Welsh counterpart of Lugh, who is master of all trades.

Luchta (LUCHT-uh)—Danaan god of carpentry.

Lugh (LOOGH)—Master of all trades. After Lugh helps the Tuatha Dé Danaan defeat the Firbolgs, he becomes their king.

Mabinogi (mab-in-O-gee)—Oldest written record of myths from the Welsh mythological tradition.

Mabon (MAB-on)—Kidnap victim whom Culhwch must find as part of his quest.

Mac Cecht (mak KECHT)—One of the three Danaan kings of Ireland at the time of the Milesian Invasion.

Mac Cuill (mak KWILL)—One of the three Danaan kings of Ireland at the time of the Milesian Invasion.

Mac Greine (mak GRAY nuh)—One of the three Danaan kings of Ireland at the time of the Milesian Invasion.

Math (MAHTH)—God who must always keep his feet on a virgin's lap.

Miach (MEE-ach)—Dian Cecht's son who crafts a real hand for Nuada.

Milesians (mill-EE-zhuns)—The first human inhabitants of Ireland.

Moytura (moy-TOO-ruh)—The Plain of Towers.

Niamh (NEE-av)—Fairy who takes Oisín to the Land of Promise.

Nuada (NOO-uh-thuh)—King of the Tuatha Dé Danaan who loses his hand during battle. When his hand is replaced with a silver one, he is no longer allowed to be king.

Ogma (OAG-muh)—Strongest man at the court of King Nuada.

Oisín (AW-sheen)—Son of Finn mac Cumaill; he is said to have first written down the stories of his father and the Fenians.

Olwen (OLE-wen)—Culhwch's true love.

Partholón (PAR-tho-lon)—King of the first inhabitants of Ireland.

Pwyll (POOH-ill)—Welsh ruler of Dyfed; he switches places with Arawn, King of the Underworld, for one year.

Rhiannon (rhee-AN-on)—Pwyll's wife.

Scáthach (SKAW-thach)—Warrior woman whom Cúchulainn fights and eventually befriends.

Sétanta (SHAY-duhn-duh)—Original named of Cúchulainn.

Síd (SHEE or SHEE<u>TH</u>)—Mounds or hills where the Tuatha Dé Danaan are said to have fled after the Milesians drove them from Ireland.

Sreng (SRENG)—Firbolg delegate at the first meeting between his people and the Tuatha Dé Danaan.

Tuatha Dé Danaan (TOO-uhth-uh day DAHN-ann)—Godlike people who inhabit Ireland before the coming of the Milesians.

Twrch Trwyth (TOORCH TROO-ith)—King who has been transformed into a boar; he keeps a comb and shears between his ears.

Úathach (OO-uh-thach)—Scathach's daughter.

Ysbaddaden Pencawr (us-buh-<u>TH</u>AH-den PEN-cower)—Fearsome giant; he is Olwen's father.

PREFACE

Who Were the Celts?

The Celts were one of the great founding cultures of European civilization. Their origins can be traced back to the second millennium B.C. The Celts' original homeland was near the headwaters of the Rhine, Rhone, and Danube Rivers, in what is now Austria, Switzerland, and Germany. By the start of the first millennium B.C., however, the Celts began a massive expansion across Europe.[1]

Over the next seven hundred years, the Celts conquered much of Europe. By the sixth century B.C., they had invaded regions of France, Spain, Austria, and Bohemia (now the Czech Republic). They also moved westward into the British Isles. In the fourth century, the Celts met up with two other great European empires— the Etruscans of Italy and Macedonia's Alexander the Great. The Celts defeated the Etruscans and even sacked Rome circa 390–387 B.C. Their meeting with Alexander the Great was a more peaceful conference. After his death, though, they invaded Greece, attacking the great shrine at Delphi. The Celts then moved to Turkey and established the area there known as Galatia.[2]

In the last three centuries B.C., the mighty Roman Empire began to check the Celts' expansion. In fact, by the first century B.C., the Romans had pushed the Celts out of continental Europe altogether. Many of the surviving Celts retreated to the British Isles. But by around 55 B.C., the Romans made their way to Britain, as well. The famous Julius Caesar led this expedition. The only areas of Britain not to be conquered were Ireland and the Isle of Man. The Romans occupied Britain for nearly five centuries. In that

Gold Armlets

Wooden Idol

white horse over 370 feet long cut into rock hilltop

ISLE of MAN

Bronze Cauldron

SCOTLAND

NORWAY

Atlantic Ocean

IRELAND

British Isles

North Sea

DENMARK

SWED

England

Brittany and Cornwall

BRITAIN

ANGLO-SAXONS

NETHERLANDS

Balt

BELGIUM

Rhine R.

GERMANY

LUXEMBOURG

FRANCE

Gaul

FRANKS

Danube R.

CZECH REPUBL

Rhone R.

SWITZERLAND

burial site

EURO

AUSTRIA

YUGOSL

PORTUGAL

SPAIN

ITALY

Rome

Mediterranean Sea

AFRICA

SICILY

N

W   E

S

MAP of CELTS

war
god
statue

stone
statue

RUSSIA

ea

RUSSIA

Gold
drinking horn

POLAND

BOHEMIA

HUNGARY

ROMANIA

BULGARIA

animal
statue

MACEDONIA

Delphi
GREECE

TURKEY
Galatia

Mediterranean Sea

celtic god
in silver

AFRICA

time, the dominating Romans displaced much of the Celts' language, culture, and customs with their own.

The Roman Empire began to decline in the third and fourth centuries A.D. By the fifth century, Roman Britain had collapsed altogether. Following this fall, Germanic tribes made their way westward into Britain. The Franks moved into Gaul, establishing France, and the Anglo-Saxon tribes created England from the formerly Celtic Britain. Over time, the Celts were pushed into remote areas such as Wales and Scotland by invading tribes and cultures.

The Celts today refer less to an ethnic or national group, but a linguistic one—meaning one connected by language. Only six Celtic language groups have survived to modern times. The Gaelic-speaking branch consists of people from Ireland, Highland Scotland, and the Isle of Man (off the Northwest coast of England). The Brythonic-speaking branch is made up of people from Wales, Brittany, and Cornwall (the southwestern area of England). Of course, not all the people from these areas still speak a Celtic language. Of the 16.5 million people who live in these places, it is estimated that only 2.5 million speak a Celtic language.[3] The Celtic myths available today stem mostly from the Irish and Welsh linguistic traditions.

Religion

Understanding the Celts' own religion, as well as the influences of outside religions, is critical to an understanding of Celtic mythology. The Celts themselves were pagan. Celtic paganism was polytheistic, which means they worshiped multiple gods. Paganism was generally very connected to nature. The pagans personified the most powerful forces of nature into gods and goddesses. Some of the forces worshiped included the sky, the sun, fertility, the sea, and the earth.

The religious leaders of the tribes were known as druids. Druids also served as teachers, advisors, lawyers, and more. Because they were considered such important members of the community, they were exempt from having to serve in the army or pay taxes. Any decisions druids arrived at were considered final and were not subject to debate.[4]

Much of what we know of druidic paganism comes from the observations and writings of Roman conquerors such as Julius Caesar. For example, it is from Caesar that we know the Celts believed in the immortality of the soul.

> As one of their leading dogmas [beliefs] they inculcate this: that souls are not annihilated, but pass after death from one body to another, and they hold that by this teaching men are much encouraged to valour, through disregarding the fear of death.[5]

Caesar also wrote of a more brutal aspect of druidic paganism: human sacrifice. He wrote of the druids:

> All the Gauls are . . . much given to superstition, and, therefore, persons afflicted by severe illness or involved in wars and dangers either make human sacrifices or vow to do so, and use the Druids as their ministers in these ceremonies.[6]

At the beginning of their conquest, the Romans were themselves polytheistic, although they believed in a different set of gods than the Celts did. Once established in Britain, the Romans worked to rid the Celts of their religion. As the religious leaders, the druids were particularly vulnerable to the religious cleansing of the Romans. Many druids were killed off in an effort to convert the masses.

Beginning in the first century A.D., however, Christianity began to gain favor in the Roman Empire. Christianity is a monotheistic religion, or a religion that worships only one, all-powerful god. By the second century A.D., Christianity became increasingly popular in Britain, although it was still not the dominant religion. Ironically, as the Roman Empire declined, the religion they had imported steadily gained in popularity. By the fifth century, missionary activity made Christianity more popular than paganism. In Ireland, for example, nearly the entire population had been converted by the singular efforts of one man—the famous St. Patrick.[7]

Celtic Myth and Literature

Throughout the Celts' existence, stories of their rich folklore and history had been passed down orally from generation to generation. Traveling poets and minstrels, known as bards, made their way throughout the Celtic world. According to some scholars, bards wandered freely and over great distances from tribe to tribe in order to share stories and myths. In this way, legends from Ireland, for example, made their way to Scotland and the Isle of Man.[8] As a result of the myths of different Celtic people continuously intermixing, aspects of the different linguistic groups' stories often resemble one another.

Celtic myths and legends were not first transcribed to manuscript form until the early Christian period. However, the people setting the stories down were Christian monks. The monks, of course, had their own agenda for Britain— to convert the Celts from paganism. Many of the original pagan elements in Celtic myths were either deleted or rewritten with a Christianized slant.

Admittedly, then, the surviving myths from the Celtic world may not be the fully authentic versions they once were. Even so, they offer valuable insight into the rich culture and customs of a nearly three-thousand-year-old people.

1

THE COMING OF THE TUATHA DÉ DANAAN

INTRODUCTION

In the collected myths of nearly every culture is a story that accounts for the origins of the universe. The ancient Egyptians, for example, tell of Earth being formed once Shu, the goddess of air, and Tefnut, the god of moisture, joined in marriage. According to Norse mythology, Midgard, or the place where human beings make their home, was formed from the eyebrows of a giant named Ymir. And the Cherokee tribe of North America believed an ancient buzzard shaped Earth's mountains and valleys from clay it had gathered from the bottom of the sea. The Gaelic Celts, too, have a story for the beginning of things. These myths differ from those of other cultures, however, in that they are not concerned with the origin of the world in general, but rather of the origin of their own country.

The first mysterious invaders of Ireland arrived at a time when the country consisted of only one treeless, grassless plain; three lakes; and nine rivers.[1] These creatures were led by Partholón, who brought with him his queen and other followers—twenty-four males and twenty-four females. They came to Ireland from the underworld and lived there for three hundred years. In that time, the land stretched out, making room for new plains and lakes. Partholón was constantly doing battle with a strange race of beings called the Fomori, who had always inhabited Ireland. Partholón and his followers managed to drive the Fomori to the northernmost corners of the country. Eventually, the strange race of Partholón was wiped out by a plague. Only one member of their tribe survived to tell their story.

Other races invaded Ireland, as well. All came from the underworld and all were forced to do battle with the

Fomori. The most important invaders of Ireland, however, were the people of Danu, or the Tuatha Dé Danaan. Danu was the mother of the gods. When her people came to Ireland, they brought with them many gifts and treasures. The following story tells more of the Tuatha Dé Danaan and their legacy to Ireland.

THE COMING OF THE TUATHA DÉ DANAAN

The Tuatha Dé Danaan arrived in Ireland on a cloud from the four great cities of fairyland.[2] While in their homelands, they had learned the arts of poetry and science. They brought these gifts, plus great treasures from the fairy cities, to their new home. The treasures included a stone that confirmed the rightful king by roaring when he stood upon it, a sword that could never be broken, a magic spear, and a pot that could feed an army without ever going empty.

After three days, the cloud on which the Danaans arrived vanished. When the air cleared, the Firbolgs, a misshapen and stupid race who lived in Ireland, realized they were no longer alone. They sent a warrior named Sreng to question the newcomers. Likewise, the Danaans sent a representative from their side.

When the two ambassadors met, each was in awe of the other's weapons. The Danaans' spears were light and sharply pointed, while those of the Firbolgs were heavy and blunt. The pair decided to exchange weapons so that each tribe could learn more about the other. Just as the pair was leaving, the Danaan ambassador suggested the Firbolgs and Danaans should split the country into two

equal halves and join to defend it against any future invaders.

Sreng returned to the Firbolg camp and told Eochaid, the king, of the Danaan ambassador's offer. Eochaid worried that if they gave the Danaans half of Ireland, they would soon want the whole. Plus, the Firbolgs were greedy and did not want to share the land with anyone. Rather than agreeing to the Danaans' offer, Eochaid refused, deciding that it would be better to declare war instead.

The two tribes met at Moytura, or the Tower of Plains, to wage their battle. The fighting was vicious. Nuada, the king of the Danaans, lost his hand while fighting with a Firbolg. The Firbolg ruler, Eochaid, was even more unfortunate—he was killed while leading a party in search of water. Once Eochaid was dead, the Danaans proved much more powerful than their opponents. The Firbolgs realized they would be defeated altogether if they continued fighting. Rather than risk a complete loss, they decided to make an agreement with the Danaans. The Danaans offered the Firbolgs one-fifth of the country. From that day, the Firbolgs made their home in the area of Ireland known as Connaught and seldom bothered the Danaans.

After the battle, Nuada should have remained ruler. There was an ancient law, though, that declared no maimed person could sit on the throne of Ireland. Nuada had a beautiful silver hand made in the hope that he would be allowed to remain king. However, the people still considered it a fake and forced him to step down.

Given the troubles with the Firbolgs, the Danaans thought it might be a wise diplomatic decision to ally with the Fomori, a race of giants that lived under the sea. They chose to ask Bres, son of the Fomori king and a Danaan mother, if he would be their ruler. He agreed. As it turned out, though, Bres was a terrible king. He was oppressive and mean and taxed the Danaans heavily. Bres also lacked generosity and hospitality—two of the worst offenses an Irish ruler could commit.[3]

While Bres tormented the Danaans, Nuada, who was now nicknamed "Of the Silver Hand," wondered if there was anything he could do. When he had lost his hand, it was Dian Cécht, the god of medicine, who had crafted the silver hand. It turned out that Dian Cécht's son, Miach, was an even greater healer. Nuada decided to visit Miach to see if he could help him with his hand. The son was able to do what the father was not—he made a real hand grow for Nuada. When the people of Ireland heard that Nuada was no longer maimed, they rejoiced. They asked him to reclaim his rightful position as king, which he did.

Bres, of course, was not happy about losing the throne. He returned to his home under the sea, where he complained to his father, Elatha. Elatha granted his son a great army which he could use to reclaim his place on the throne. He also advised his son to seek the help of Balor— the greatest and most evil of Fomori kings. Balor was nicknamed "of the Evil Eye" because only one glance from his great eye could strike down all who looked upon it. In his old age, Balor's eye became droopy and the lid had to be hoisted up by his servants with ropes and pulleys. Even so, Balor's evil eye was a great weapon.

Nuada and the Danaans grew nervous when they heard news of Bres and Balor's alliance. They knew they would be no match for the powerful Balor. In fact, Balor's only weakness was an ancient prophecy that he would be killed by his own grandson. But Balor had taken care to kill all his only daughter's offspring, so even this path seemed hopeless.

The Danaans assembled at the royal palace of Tara to determine what they could do. While there, a stranger arrived at the palace. He was greeted by the gatekeeper, who asked the stranger his profession. No one was admitted without being the master of some craft.

"I am a carpenter," said the stranger.

The gatekeeper replied that the king already had a skilled carpenter and had no need of another.

"Then tell the king I am a master smith."

"We already have a smith," answered the gatekeeper.

"Then I am a warrior, too," said the stranger.

"We do not need one," replied the gatekeeper. "The great Ogma is our champion."[4]

The stranger went on to name all the professions and arts he could think of—poet, harpist, scientist, physician, sorcerer, sculptor. Each time he was told that the king already had such a man at court.

"Then ask the king," said the stranger, "if he has with him a man of all these crafts at once, for if he has, there is no need for me at Tara."[5]

When the king heard this news, he was intrigued. He decided to test the stranger. Nuada sent his best chess champion to play the man. The stranger won quickly, inventing a new move in the process. With the victory, Nuada offered him an invitation to the palace. As he walked in, the stranger saw Ogma, the King's champion, pushing a stone so large it would take eighty oxen to pull it.[6] The stranger helped Ogma by effortlessly lifting the great rock and putting it in its place.

All the people at the palace were amazed by the stranger's show of strength and intelligence. They wondered if he was also a great musician, and asked him to play upon his harp for them. First, the stranger played a lullaby that made the crowd fall asleep for two days. Next,

he played a song so sad they all began to weep. Finally, he played a joyous song, to which they all cheered and danced.

Nuada and his people were all awed. They wondered if the beautiful man might be of help in fighting the Fomori. As it turned out, the stranger would be more than just some help. He revealed that he was Lugh, Master of All Arts. His father was the Danaan Cian, his mother was the Fomor Ethlinn, but most importantly, his grandfather was none other than Balor! Although Balor believed he had protected himself from the prophecy by killing his grandchildren, he was unaware that one child, Lugh, had been rescued from death and raised in secret.

Lugh agreed to help the Danaans in their defense against the Fomori. Before he led them into battle, though, Lugh believed they needed certain magical instruments and tools to ensure victory. He dispatched messengers, soldiers, and servants across the land on various quests. In total, it took seven years to gather everything they needed. But in the end, the Danaans had collected several magic items to help them in battle. A magical pig's skin, for example, healed every wound or sickness it touched. Seven swine provided unlimited food for the Danaans. With these items and more in hand, the Danaans were ready to take on the Fomori.

The giants and the gods met at the Tower of Plains— the same site of the Danaans' battle against the Firbolgs. They fought hand-to-hand for days on end. The fighting itself was equal, but the results were not. While the Danaans lost as many men and weapons as the Fomori, their numbers never seemed to dwindle. This was because of the gods' magic and the items they had brought with them. Each time a Danaan spear broke, Goibhniu, the smith god, hammered out a new spearhead with only three blows of his mallet. Luchtar, God of Carpentry, would instantly make a new handle. Likewise, wounds were healed by the pig skin or by the powers of Dian Cécht, the god of medicine.

The lack of results only infuriated the Fomori further. They charged the Danaans with a great shout. Swords clashed, shields shattered, and darts whistled by. In desperation, the Fomori brought out Balor, hoping to finish off their enemies once and for all. Balor struck down many Danaans, including Nuada of the Silver Hand. At last, he met up with Lugh. He ordered his servants to pull up his great eyelid. But while the lid was only partially open, Lugh took a slingshot and hurled a great stone. It struck Balor's mighty eye and lodged deep in his brain. Balor fell dead, fulfilling the prophecy that he would die at his grandson's hand.

With Balor dead, the Danaans quickly defeated the Fomori. Lugh, who had led them to their victory, was made king at the battle's end.

QUESTIONS AND ANSWERS

Q: *What four gifts did the Tuatha Dé Danaan bring from their fairy home?*

A: The Tuatha Dé Danaan brought with them a stone that confirmed the rightful king by roaring when he stood upon it, a sword that could never be broken, a magic spear, and a pot that could feed an army without ever going empty.

Q: *How were the weapons of the Firbolgs different than those of the Danaans?*

A: The Firbolgs' weapons were heavy and blunt, while the Danaans' spears were light and sharply pointed.

Q: *Why was Nuada not allowed to be king after the battle with the Firbolgs?*

A: Nuada was not allowed to be king because he had lost his hand in battle and there was an ancient law that said no maimed man could be king.

Q: *What was Balor's most powerful weapon?*

A: Balor had an "evil eye" that struck dead all those who looked upon it.

Q: *What could Lugh offer that no one else at Nuada's court could?*

A: Lugh was a master of all skills at once.

Q: *Why did the Danaans never run out of weapons while fighting the Fomori?*

A: The Danaans never ran out of weapons because Goibhniu, the Blacksmith God, and Luchtar, the God of

Carpentry, instantly made a new weapon each time one broke.

Q: *What was the ancient prophecy that Balor feared? Did it come to pass?*

A: Balor believed a prophecy that he would be killed by his own grandson. Although he thought he had killed the children of his only daughter, one of his grandsons had been rescued and raised in secret. This was Lugh, who eventually killed Balor by hurling a stone into his eye with a slingshot. The prophecy had been fulfilled.

EXPERT COMMENTARY

The Tuatha Dé Danaan represent the importance of certain values in Celtic culture, such as science, poetry, and artistic skill. In their battle with the Firbolgs, their victory represents a greater triumph of the forces of good and intelligence over those of dullness and ignorance. The contrast of the Firbolgs' heavy, blunt weapons to the sharp, light spears of the Danaans makes this metaphor clearer.

The battle with the Fomori is a bit more complicated to interpret. In this part of the myth, the powers of the gods come up against not exactly evil, but the negative forces of the universe in general. According to Alexi Kondratiev, the Fomori symbolize "the powers of the Land itself, givers of both fertility and blight—but indiscriminately, with no regard for the welfare of humans.[7] T. W. Rolleston offers a slightly different interpretation:

> Again in their [the Danaans'] struggle with a far more powerful and dangerous enemy, the Fomorians, we are evidently to see the combat of the powers of Light with evil of a more positive kind than represented by the Firbolgs. The Fomorians stand not for mere dullness or stupidity, but for the forces of tyranny, cruelty, and greed—for moral, rather than for intellectual darkness.[8]

The Gaelic Celts, then, did not think of their world as innately good or evil. Rather, they acknowledged that good and bad things can happen with little explanation why.

2

THE MILESIAN INVASION

INTRODUCTION

While the Danaans defeated both the Firbolgs and the Fomori, their reign in Ireland would not last forever. For all the positive values they represented, the one thing they could never be was human. The myth of the Danaans may have explained how science, art, and knowledge came to Ireland, but it did not explain the origin of mortal people. It would take another myth—the story of the coming of the Milesians—to provide such an explanation.

The Celts believed the Milesians most closely resembled human beings in their current form. Even so, they had their origin in a somewhat mystical background. According to a purely Celtic tradition, human beings are descendents of Bíle, the God of the underworld. Human beings arrived from the land of the dead to make a new home in the present world.

As the myth was retold and eventually recorded by Christian storytellers, some of the pagan elements were rewritten. In Christianized versions of the Milesian invasion, human beings did not arrive from the supernatural world of the dead, but rather from Spain. As the original and edited version of the myths became more and more intertwined, "Spain" came to be synonymous with the land of the dead.

THE MILESIAN INVASION

In "Spain," a man named Bregon built a very tall watchtower. Bregon's son, Ith, liked to climb the tower and look out over the sea. One very clear winter's day, he noticed a land he had never seen before. Ith decided he wanted to explore it further, so he set sail with ninety warriors for the strange new land.

The land Ith had seen was, of course, Ireland. At that time, there were three Danaan kings—Mac Cuill, Mac Cecht, and Mac Greine—who ruled Ireland. As Ith landed, he noticed the three rulers arguing. They were bickering over how to divide the country. Seeing the stranger approach, the kings asked Ith to help them decide. Ith had no practical advice, but instead told the kings to act according to the laws of justice.[1] He then praised the country for its moderate climate and abundance of good food, such as fish, wheat, honey, and fruit. When the kings heard the newcomer, they began to worry that he was plotting to overtake their country. They killed him on the spot, but spared his followers, who were allowed to return to Spain with the body.

The people of Spain were furious to learn of Ith's death. His nephew, Mil Espaine, determined to go to Ireland to

avenge his death. He set sail with his family and thirty-six chiefs and their families. Among the Milesians, as they came to be known, was Mil Espaine's son, Amairgin. Amairgin was a poet and a powerful druid, or magician. Upon landing on the Irish coast, Amairgin recited a poem, asking the land and its resources to side with Mil Espaine and his followers.

The group made their way to Tara, the capital and palace of the Danaans. A short way into their march, they met up with Banba, the wife of Mac Cuill. Banba greeted the Milesians warmly. While she was not happy to hear they had arrived to conquer Ireland, she asked that the island be named after her should they win. Amairgin promised it would be so. Further along, the Milesians met up with another goddess, Fotla, wife of Mac Cecht. She made the same request as Banba. Amairgin again responded that it would be so.

Finally, as the group proceeded to the center of the island, they met Eriu, wife of Mac Greine. Eriu greeted the Milesians most warmly of all. She welcomed the group to the fair island and prophesized that the human race would be the most perfect the land would ever know. She turned to Amairgin. Like Banba and Fotla, she asked that the island bear her name should the Milesians be successful in their battle. Amairgin answered that Eriu would be the country's principal name. (While all three names have been used to describe Ireland, it is only *Eriu*, or Erin in a different form, that remains as a poetic nickname for the island.)

After leaving Eriu, the Milesians made the last leg of their journey to Tara. There, they found Mac Cuill, Mac Cecht, and Mac Greine waiting for them. The kings and other Danaans complained that the humans had not followed the laws of warfare. According to ancient

traditions, invaders were required to give the inhabitants of a country advance notice of an attack. The Milesians admitted that they had not done this.

To settle the matter, the two sides decided to present their case to Amairgin. The Danaans had great respect for the druid. Even so, they threatened to kill him immediately if his decision obviously favored the Milesians. After careful consideration, Amairgin came to a verdict, which was considered the first judgment ever delivered in Ireland.[2] He agreed that the Milesians acted unfairly and took the Danaans by surprise. To make up for this, the Milesians had to retreat out to sea the length of nine waves. If they were able to return to shore, they would have rightfully earned the land as their own.

Both sides felt Amairgin's judgment was a fair one. The Milesians retreated to their ship and sailed nine wave lengths back from the shore. Once the signal was given to attack, the Milesians began paddling. Despite their immense effort, however, the Milesians realized they were not making any progress. Unbeknownst to them, the gods had combined all their powers to create a strong wind to keep the Milesians in place.

At first the Milesians thought it might be a natural storm that was hindering them. They sent a man to climb the highest mast to see if the wind was indeed caused by a storm. The man quickly climbed up and then back down. He reported that no storm could be seen on the horizon and that the wind must therefore be supernatural in origin. Amairgin quickly took control of the situation. He chanted a poem that called out to the powers of the land itself—powers far greater than even those of the gods. The land of Ireland responded to Amairgin's spell and the winds soon died down.

The Milesians continued to shore. Once they landed,

Amairgin called out to the sea, as he had done with the land. With these forces behind them, the humans began their assault on the gods. The three Danaan kings and their wives were killed in battle. The Milesian invasion was successful and they took over rule of the country.

While the Danaans were defeated, however, they did not withdraw from Ireland altogether. Using their magical powers, they made themselves invisible to the majority of humans. From that day forward, Ireland was divided into two realms—the earthly and the spiritual. While the humans ruled the earthly domain, the Danaans dwelled silently and invisibly in the spirit world. They made their homes under mounds or hills, known as *síd*. The gods became known as "the people of the hills." Every male god was imagined as a *Fear-síd*, meaning "man of the hill." Goddesses were called *Ban-síd*, or "woman of the hill." Over the years, the words have evolved into their present forms: "fairy" and "banshee." Both of these characters remain popular in Irish folklore today.

QUESTIONS AND ANSWERS

Q: *How did Ith first see Ireland?*

A: Ith first saw Ireland from the top of a tall watchtower in Spain.

Q: *Why did the three kings of Ireland kill Ith?*

A: The three kings killed Ith after he praised their country because they were afraid he was plotting to overtake it himself.

Q: *What did each of the three queens ask of the Milesians?*

A: Each queen asked that the island be named after her should the Milesians succeed in their quest to conquer Ireland.

Q: *Why did the Danaans feel the Milesians' initial invasion was unfair?*

A: According to ancient traditions, invaders were required to give the inhabitants of a country advance notice of an attack. The Milesians had not done this.

Q: *How did Amairgin help the Milesians conquer the storm that the Danaans had created?*

A: Amairgin invoked the power of Ireland itself in order to quiet the storm.

Q: *What happened to the Tuatha Dé Danaan after the Milesians had defeated them?*

A: The Danaans made themselves invisible to human eyes and retreated to live under the hills and mounds of Ireland.

EXPERT COMMENTARY

Amairgin plays a crucial role in the Milesians' defeat of the Danaans. In that way, he illustrates the importance of the druid in ancient Celtic culture. Druids were much more than magicians or poets, however. According to Peter Berresford Ellis, druids:

> were accounted philosophers, natural scientists, and teachers and, more importantly, were able to give legal, political, and even military judgments. They were trained in "international law" as well as tribal law. They could prevent warfare between tribes, for their moral and legal authority was greater than that of chieftains or kings. Even the High King could not speak at an assembly before his druid had spoken.[3]

As Christianity penetrated Celtic lands, pagan druids were looked down on. Even so, they did not disappear altogether. In fact, many scholars contend that "the early saints were druids" presented in a Christianized package.[4]

3

CÚCHULAINN AND EMER

INTRODUCTION

Like most countries, ancient Ireland was divided into different geographical areas, in this case known as provinces. One of the more famous of these provinces is Ulster, located on the northernmost end of the island. Ulster still exists in Ireland today and comprises part of what is known as Northern Ireland.

The stories surrounding this province are known collectively as the Red Branch or Ulster Cycle. The Red Branch myths were recorded sometime in the twelfth century, but it is believed that they were passed down orally for nearly a thousand years before they were written down.[1] This series of myths has always been and continues to be widely known in Celtic mythology, in part because of the popularity of the main hero, Cúchulainn.

As a child, Cúchulainn was known as Sétanta. He was the nephew and foster son of King Conchobar, but his maternal grandfather was said to be Dagda, the father of all the gods, and his father was Lugh, the sun god. With or without his divine bloodline, it was clear from the time he was young that Sétanta was destined to be a great warrior. At the age of seven, for example, Sétanta was on his way to a feast in the king's honor when he was attacked by the hound of Culann, the king's blacksmith. Although the terrible hound was as fierce as one hundred regular dogs, Sétanta immediately killed the beast by hurling a ball at its throat.

The king and his subjects were surprised that the young boy had survived such an attack. Culann, however, was upset that his great hound was dead. Even though he was young, Sétanta proved he was not only strong and brave, but also honorable. He offered to train a puppy to

replace the dog he had killed. In the meantime, Sétanta offered to fulfill the role of the hound himself, guarding Culann's house and protecting him from enemies. From that day forward he was called *Cúchulainn*, which means "Culann's hound."

The next story is just one of many that describes the adventures of Cúchulainn and his companions, the Champions of the Red Branch. In it, he overcomes many obstacles to win the beautiful Emer for his wife. Cúchulainn's adventures give a sense of the traits most important in the Ulster Cycle, such as bravery, cunning, and strength. Another notable element of the myth is its depiction of strong women—not only does Cúchulainn pursue women, he battles them and matches wits with them, as well.

Cúchulainn and Emer

As Cúchulainn grew older he became increasingly more handsome. A mere glance at any woman was enough to make her fall instantly in love with him. The men of Ulster became worried that Cúchulainn would entice away their wives with his good looks, so they demanded he find a wife of his own. A party was formed and sent to the furthest corners of Ireland, but even after a full year, they could not find a woman Cúchulainn found suitable.[2] At last, Cúchulainn came across Emer, daughter of Forgall. She possessed all six "gifts" by which women were judged: the gifts of beauty, voice, sweet speech, needlework, wisdom, and chastity.[3]

When Cúchulainn first approached Emer, she laughed at his advances, saying that he was too young. Ignoring her dismissals, Cúchulainn admired her beauty aloud. Emer replied that no man would ever possess her beauty before slaying hundreds of men and making his name known across Ireland. Cúchulainn pledged to do just that, provided that Emer would agree to marry him once he succeeded in his quest. Emer agreed, so Cúchulainn went off to win his fame and fortune, stopping at King Conchobar's palace on the way.

Emer's father, Forgall, was not pleased with these arrangements, however. He had had a premonition that his daughter's marriage to Cúchulainn would somehow lead to his own death. To guard against such a fate, he wanted to make sure that Cúchulainn would not survive his adventures. He disguised himself as a traveler and followed Cúchulainn to the king's court. There, he watched Cúchulainn and the other Champions of the Red Branch demonstrate their skill and strength before their king.

Still disguised, Forgall approached the king and said loud enough to be overheard that Cúchulainn's skill was impressive. It would be even greater, Forgall continued, if Cúchulainn made his way to the island of Alba to study the craft of war under Scáthach the Amazon, the fiercest female warrior in the world.[4] Forgall knew that Cúchulainn, who prided himself on being the best at everything, would not be able to resist such a challenge. Sure enough, Cúchulainn declared he would indeed make his way to Alba. Forgall secretly hoped that Cúchulainn would be killed in the process.

Cúchulainn made his way to Alba, the Island of Shadows. He faced many perils along the way. When he finally arrived, he was faced with the Bridge of Leaps, which offered the only passage onto the island. The treacherous bridge was very long and worked something like a see-saw—whenever weight was added to one side, the other end lifted up until the entire bridge stood straight up in the air. Three times Cúchulainn tried to cross, and three times he failed.

Perhaps because of his divine relatives, Cúchulainn was blessed with a few seemingly-super human powers. When he got very angry, for example, his rage would build up inside him to the point that he would grow hot and almost glow. With this extra energy, Cúchulainn was able to perform "the hero's salmon leap," which enabled him to jump huge distances. After failing three times to cross the bridge, Cúchulainn became enraged and did his salmon leap directly onto the middle of the bridge. He reached the far end of the bridge so quickly that it did not have time to spring back on him.

Cúchulainn did not realize it, but he was being watched by Scáthach and her daughter, Úathach, as he crossed the bridge and approached their home. Upon seeing the beautiful young man, Úathach fell immediately in love with him. She went to greet him at the door. But Cúchulainn wasted little time with Úathach and demanded right away to know where Scáthach was. Overcome with love, Úathach not only told him where to find her mother, but the secret way to force her to grant whatever he wished, as well.[5] Úathach revealed that Scáthach was up in a yew tree with her two sons. If Cúchulainn were to surprise her and quickly draw his sword on her, she would promise him anything in return for her life.

So, Cúchulainn performed the hero's salmon leap straight up into the highest branches of the tree. He drew his sword on Scáthach and placed its point on her breast. He threatened to kill her if she did not take him as her student. Wanting to be spared a painful death, Scáthach promised to teach him all she knew.

Cúchulainn stayed with Scáthach for a year and a day, learning the art of battle and the techniques of war.[6] Cúchulainn was such a good student that Scáthach presented him with the *gae bolga*—a terrible weapon that made only one wound when entering, but exploded into thirty small barbs once inside the enemy's body.[7]

Cúchulainn's new skills were soon put to use on the

island. Scáthach was at the time at war with Aife, queen of another tribe on the island and an equally fierce warrior. The day of the great fight, Scáthach tried to prevent Cúchulainn from fighting, thinking that the terrible Aife would surely kill him. Scáthach gave him a sleeping potion so that he would not be awake during the battles. But the potion, which was strong enough to last thirty-six hours on any normal man, only lasted one hour on Cúchulainn.

As soon as he awoke, he went to join the fight.[8] He arrived just in time to discover Aife had challenged Scáthach to single combat. Cúchulainn demanded to go in his teacher's place, but first asked Scáthach to tell him what Aife valued most in the world. Scáthach answered that Aife prized her two horses, her chariot, and her charioteer above all else.

Cúchulainn and Aife began to fight, and at first it appeared that the young man was no match for the fierce woman warrior. With just one blow, she shattered Cúchulainn's sword. But at the very moment it looked like she would kill him, Cúchulainn called out "Look! Aife's chariot and horses have fallen into the valley! They are all dead!" When Aife turned around to see what had happened to her beloved possessions, Cúchulainn grabbed her and put a knife to her throat. He offered to spare her life only if she pledged peace with Scáthach and offered hostages as proof of the agreement. Aife agreed and peace was returned to the island.

In the meantime, Emer was at home warding off potential suitors. Word that Emer might be forced to marry another made its way back to Cúchulainn on Alba.[9] Not wanting to lose his bride, Cúchulainn decided that it was time to return home to Ireland. Forgall, of course, was dismayed to learn that not only had Cúchulainn survived his adventure, but that he was returning an even stronger warrior than before. Forgall took great pains to guard his home against any attacks.

The barricades Forgall put up were so strong that it took Cúchulainn a full year just to reach the wall of the fortress. When he finally got there he leaped over the high walls, killing eight men with each stroke of his blade.[10] Forgall was among those slain.[11] Cúchulainn quickly grabbed Emer and her foster sister, along with their weight in silver and gold, then performed another of his salmon leaps to make their escape.

As they began to ride away, they heard a loud cry and saw Forgall's sister, Scenmed, following them with a troop of men to avenge her fallen brother. Cúchulainn killed her on the spot, which has been known ever since as the Ford Scenmed. Scenmed's men continued to chase the hero, but at Glondath, Cúchulainn killed one hundred of them with ease. Emer praised her love for his great deed and declared the place would be called Glondath, the Ford of Deeds, forevermore.

Cúchulainn and the women continued riding, coming eventually to Rae Bann, the White Plain. Once again they were attacked and once again Cúchulainn slaughtered his assailants. As streams of his enemies' blood ran over the once-white plains, Emer said the place would henceforth be known as Crúfóit, Sod of Blood.[12] Finally, the group reached another ford near Boinne. At this place, Cúchulainn chased his enemies northward, with the sod, or grass, from his horses' hooves flying all over the ford. He then repeated his action in the opposite direction, spraying the ford with sod toward the south. From that day on, the place has been known as the Ford of Two Sods.

With no enemies left to conquer, Cúchulainn and Emer were free to marry. They never parted again.

QUESTIONS AND ANSWERS

Q: *Why did* Sétanta *become known as Cúchulainn?*

A: After killing Culann's prized hound, Sétanta not only offered to train a puppy to replace the dog, but to fulfill the dog's role himself until the pup was ready. From then on, he was known as Cúchulainn, which means Culann's hound.

Q: *What were the six gifts that women were judged by and how many of these did Emer possess?*

A: The gifts women were judged by were: beauty, voice, sweet speech, needlework, wisdom, and chastity. Emer possessed all six of these gifts.

Q: *How did Forgall trick Cúchulainn into leaving on a journey?*

A: Disguised as a traveler, Forgall commented that Cúchulainn had impressive skills, but would be even better if he studied under Scáthach. Forgall knew Cúchulainn would not be able to resist the challenge.

Q: *What unique skill did Cúchulainn use to pass the Bridge of Leaps?*

A: Cúchulainn was able to leap great distances. This skill was called the hero's salmon leap.

Q: *How did Cúchulainn conquer Aife in battle?*

A: Cúchulainn tricked Aife into looking away by telling her that her prized chariot and horses had fallen into a valley. As soon as she turned, Cúchulainn grabbed her and put a knife to her throat.

Q: *What evidence remains from Cúchulainn's battles with Scenmed and her men?*

A: The names of the geographical places where Cúchulainn fought were changed to reflect his victories. After spilling his enemies' blood over the White Plain, for example, it became known as the Sod of Blood instead.

EXPERT COMMENTARY

In the course of this story many real places are mentioned. Thomas Kinsella describes how this technique was often employed in the Ulster myths to explain the origin of certain places' names:

> Place-names and their frequently fanciful meanings and origins occupy a remarkable place [in these myths] by modern standards. It is often enough justification for the inclusion of an incident that it ends in the naming of some physical feature; certain incidents indeed seem to have been invented merely to account for a place-name.[13]

Other mythologists have attempted to identify the real-life counterparts to the fictional places named in the myths. The fictional island of Alba, for example, where Scáthach is reputed to have lived, is widely identified with the island of Skye, a large island off the coast of Northwest Scotland. In fact, T. W. Rolleston points out that on the island of Skye, "the Cuchulain Peaks still bear witness to the legend."[14]

The inclusion of real place-names has also led scholars to wonder about the possible real-life identities of the characters. The supernatural powers of a character such as Cúchulainn are obviously elements of pure myth. Even so, some scholars argue that some characters are based on real-life people. In answering the question, "History or mythology?" Charles Squire, for example, writes that it is:

> A mingling perhaps of both. Cúchulainn may have been the name of a real Gaelic warrior, however suspiciously he may now resemble the sun god, who is said to have been his father. King Conchobar may have been the real chief of a tribe of Irish Celts before he became an adumbration [a representation] of the Gaelic sky-god.[15]

4

OISÍN

INTRODUCTION

Long after Cúchulainn and his followers died, a new group of heroes emerged in Ireland. In this next cycle of myths, supposedly set in the third century A.D., the central character is a man named Fionn Mac Cumaill. The Anglicized version of his name, which is slightly more well known, is Finn Mac Cool. The stories surrounding Finn and the Fianna, a band of warriors who followed Finn, are collectively called the Fenian cycle.

Like Cúchulainn and the Champions of the Red Branch, Finn and the men of the Fianna patrolled Ireland to protect against invaders. They encountered many exciting adventures along the way. Unlike the Ultonians, however, members of the Fianna were not only expert warriors, but learned, cultured men of poetry and science. Finn, for example, was as wise as he was fearless.

Finn's real name was Demna. He was nicknamed Finn, or "the fair one," because of his pale skin and golden-blond hair. Finn spent years learning to become a great warrior, but realized that he wanted to study science and the arts, too. He decided to study under a great druid named Finegas.

Finegas lived by a deep pool where the "salmon of knowledge" swam. These magical fish were the source of all knowledge in the universe. It was prophesized that only a man named Finn could eat them. Once he did, he, too, would be all-knowing. Finegas assumed he was the Finn of the prophecy and spent years trying to catch a salmon. A short time after Finn arrived as his pupil, he finally succeeded.

Finegas gave the salmon to his student to cook, but warned him not to eat a bite. He left Finn to his work.

When he returned, he noticed that the boy looked somehow different. He asked Finn if he had tasted the fish. Finn replied that he had not eaten any. But, while he was cooking it, he burned his thumb on the hot pan and stuck his thumb in his mouth to cool it. Finegas realized that the boy was the Finn who was supposed to eat the fish. He told Finn to finish the entire salmon. Finn soon became one of the wisest men to ever live. From that day forward, he had only to stick his thumb in his mouth as he had when he was burned in order to receive any knowledge he wished.

But Finn was not the only extraordinary member of the Fianna. Finn's own son, Oisín, was just as great a warrior as his father. He was also a gifted poet. In fact, legend has it that he was the first person to tell and record the stories of the Fianna.

The following myth recounts some of Oisín's adventures and explores how he came to pass his story down. In this story, paganism comes up directly against Christianity. Oisín, who lives for a time in a fairy kingdom, represents the supernatural. At the end of the story, though, he meets up with Patrick. In the Christian tradition, Patrick is the famous St. Patrick, the patron saint of Ireland.

OISÍN

Like most great heroes, Oisín possessed incredible beauty. It seemed women were always falling in love with him after gazing on his perfect face. One day, while hunting with Finn and several members of the Fianna, Oisín noticed a woman riding toward them on a white horse. The beautiful maiden was dressed like royalty. She wore a gold crown on her head and a brown silk robe with red-gold stars draped over her shoulders. Even the horse on which she rode was bedecked with gold horseshoes and had a silver wreath around its head.[1]

Finn asked the woman her name. She replied that she was Niamh, daughter of Manannán Mac Lir, god of the sea and king of the Land of Promise.[2] She explained that she had come all the way from her invisible fairy home because of her love for Oisín. She asked him to return with her. Oisín immediately agreed. Finn and his companions could do nothing to stop the lovestruck young man. They watched as he climbed on to the white horse behind Niamh and wrapped his arms around her.

The pair rode for a long time—across the land and then over the tops of the waves of the sea. Along the way, Niamh described the Land of Promise as the sweetest and

dreamiest place in the universe. Oisín felt as if he were in a trance. He felt very peaceful, but lost track of time and place. Strange sights kept appearing before his eyes. He saw fairy palaces with strange towers and gateways. A hornless deer ran by slowly, chased by a white dog with one red ear. These strange dogs only existed in the "other world."

Finally, Niamh and Oisín reached the Land of Promise. While there, Oisín had a few adventures, such as saving a princess from a Fomori giant. He was blissfully happy there with Niamh. After a period of what he thought was three weeks, though, he realized he missed his father and his homeland. He asked Niamh if he could go back to visit. Niamh granted his request and even lent him her fairy horse. The only rule she had was that he could not let his feet touch earthly soil or he would never be allowed to return to the Land of Promise. Oisín promised and made his way to Ireland.

When he arrived, he found the country entirely changed. The palace of the Fianna was no longer in the same place. The men who roamed around seemed tiny compared to Oisín. He asked if anyone knew where he could find Finn and the Fianna. The only responses he received were surprised glances. He was told that those were the names of people who had lived long ago. Oisín had not been gone for three weeks as he had thought—he had been gone for three hundred years!

As Oisín was trying to figure out what to do, he noticed a group of men trying to move a great boulder. He rode over to help them. The men were in awe of the beautiful, giant man. He was stronger than all of them combined. While still in his saddle, Oisín leaned over to move the boulder. With one hand, he put it in its rightful place. The men cheered for Oisín.

Their celebrations did not last long, though. As Oisín sat back into his saddle, a strap broke and his foot hit the ground. Instantly, the white horse disappeared and the man dropped to the ground. As he stood up, the men were shocked to see not a young, strong giant, but a weak, withered, gray-haired man who was no larger than they were.

The old man seemed confused. He was babbling about Finn and asking where he could find the Fianna. Because the old man was too weak to care for himself, the men brought him to Patrick. Patrick had arrived in Ireland many years earlier. He had converted the Irish to Christianity. Rather than believing in many gods, they now believed in only one, all-powerful god.

Patrick took Oisín into his home. He treated the old man with great respect and hospitality. The two men did not see eye to eye on religion, though. Patrick tried to convert Oisín to Christianity, but Oisín always refused his arguments. The pair spent the rest of their lives debating the issue.

Despite their different beliefs, Patrick took a great interest in Oisín's stories. Oisín stayed with Patrick a long time, telling stories of the Fianna every day. Patrick suggested Oisín write down his adventures so that the stories of Finn and the Fianna could be preserved forever. Legend has it that Oisín's own transcription is how people came to know his story.

QUESTIONS AND ANSWERS

Q: *What did Finn Mac Cool do in order to gain all the knowledge he needed?*

A: Finn would stick his thumb in his mouth as he had when he was burned in order to receive any knowledge he wished.

Q: *From what land did Niamh come to find Oisín?*

A: Niamh came from the fairy country, the Land of Promise, in order to find Oisín.

Q: *How long did Oisín believe he was in the Land of Promise?*

A: Oisín believed he was in the Land of Promise for three weeks. In reality, he was there for three hundred years.

Q: *What happened when Oisín tried to move a great boulder for a group of mortal men?*

A: While Oisín was trying to move the boulder, he fell from his horse and his foot touched the ground. He immediately transformed from a young giant to a withered, frail old man.

Q: *Where did the group of mortal men take Oisín after he had changed into an old man?*

A: The men took Oisín to the home of St. Patrick.

EXPERT COMMENTARY

In large part, any present-day interest in Celtic mythology and scholarship can trace its roots to the story of Oisín and to the work of an eighteenth-century Scottish poet named James Macpherson. Beginning in 1760, Macpherson published the first of three volumes of poetry that has since become known as *Ossian* (the Scottish version of the name Oisín). His retelling of the tales of Finn and the Fianna were many people's first exposure to the myths. Macpherson claimed the works were translations from original Gaelic manuscripts.

A huge controversy ensued over the authenticity of his work. Famous writer and philosopher Samuel Johnson denounced the work as a fake. Macpherson's continual refusal to produce the manuscripts he claimed to have translated only added fuel to the fire. It seemed all of Europe was involved in the great literary debate of the century. As Paul deGategno writes, however:

> The debate has long since been definitively settled: scholars agree that Macpherson did collect a number of Gaelic Ossianic ballads, sometimes using original characters and ideas but more typically altering these, while adding modern, non-Gaelic characteristics of his own.[3]

While the poems may not have been as authentic as Macpherson claimed, the stories did capture the public's imagination. Readers from England to France and from Germany to the United States were captivated by Macpherson's *Ossian*. The interest would spawn an entire literary movement, known as Romanticism, inspiring famous poets such as William Wordsworth and Walt Whitman. Even Napoleon Bonaparte, famous French military leader and emperor, could not get enough of the stories. According to deGategno, Napoleon carried a copy of the book with him on his military campaigns.

> Napoleon believed that poetry had the power to inspire men to great deeds and to awaken the warlike spirits of a nation. At the same time, Ossian appealed to his fatalism and superstition. He understood the Celtic heroes of the poems, men driven to valorous deeds, kept alive forever by the songs of the bard.[4]

5

GWYDION AND ARANRHOD

INTRODUCTION

The other tradition of Celtic mythology stems not from Irish roots, but from Welsh ones. The name *Welsh* was given to the British Celts by the Anglo-Saxons who first invaded the area in the fifth century. The word means "foreigners," which is ironic considering the Welsh were the native inhabitants.[1]

Sadly, fewer stories from the Welsh tradition have survived than from that of the Irish. The majority of the Welsh literature has been preserved in two fourteenth-century manuscripts: *The White Book of Rhydderch* and *The Red Book of Hergest*. Collectively, the stories within these two books are known as *The Four Branches of the Mabinogi*, or simply *Mabinogion* in Welsh.

The stories of the *Mabinogi* were first recorded between the years 1300 and 1425.[2] Many scholars believe that the tales themselves originated far earlier. Some of the stories, for example, describe customs, styles, and vocabulary of a period two hundred years earlier. The *Mabinogion* was not translated into English until the nineteenth century. Lady Charlotte Elizabeth Guest first published her English translations between the years 1838 and 1849.

As in the Irish tradition, Welsh myths were passed down orally long before they were recorded in books. Traveling bards made their way from place to place sharing the stories. As a result, different versions of the stories became intermixed. Even elements of the Irish myths made their way into the Welsh ones. For example, Welsh gods and goddesses were all descended from a single mother goddess named Dôn. Dôn is herself the same divine character as Danu, and the children of Dôn are the Welsh equivalent of the Tuatha Dé Danaan. Likewise, in the following story, we are introduced to the son god Lleu Llaw Gyffes, who is the counterpart of the Irish god Lugh.

GWYDION AND ARANRHOD

Math, a Welsh god of great wealth, was burdened by a very unusual curse: he could only live if his feet were resting on a virgin's lap. When his original virgin foot-holder was abducted, Math was forced to look for a new one. Gwydion, God of illusion and magic, as well as of poetry and science, was Math's good friend. He suggested his sister, Aranrhod, for the job.

Aranrhod was very honored that she was being considered. She went before Math in order for him to test her. As it turned out, she was not a virgin at all. Much to Aranrhod's embarrassment, when Math waved his wand over her, she gave birth to two children on the spot.

One of the children was named Dylan Eil Ton, meaning "Sea, Son of the Wave."[3] The moment he was born, he plunged into the sea because he believed it was his native element. When he died many years later, at the hand of his own uncle, it is said that all the seas of Britain and Ireland wept for him.

Aranrhod's other son was rescued by Gwydion. He raised the boy as his own child. The boy grew at a very fast rate. When he was two, he was able to travel on his own.

When he was only four, he was the size of a boy twice his age.

One day, Gwydion took the boy to visit his mother. Aranrhod hated the children who had exposed her lie to Math. She was not happy that Gwydion brought the boy to her home. The only interest she showed was asking what his name was. Gwydion replied that he had not yet been named. When Aranrhod heard this she decided to lay a curse upon the boy. She proclaimed that he would never have a name until she herself gave him one. The idea of not having a name was a very serious problem. Many ancient Britons thought the name to be the same as the soul.[4] Gwydion determined to find a way to secure a name for his son.

The next day, the two went to the seashore by Aranrhod's palace. They disguised themselves as master leather craftsmen and set up a little shop on a boat. They made fine leather goods for the townspeople. After a short while, word of their great skill spread back to Aranrhod. When she heard of the craftsmen, she sent an order for a new pair of shoes.

Gwydion and his son set out to make the shoes. Although Aranrhod had given her measurements, they deliberately made the shoes too big. A servant picked up the pair and brought them back to Aranrhod. She was very angry when she tried them on and found they did not fit. She sent her servant back and had him demand the shoes be made again. The second time Gwydion and the boy crafted a pair that were intentionally too small. When Aranrhod received another pair in the wrong size, she was furious. She made her way to the shore to have an exact measurement of her foot taken. She would then wait herself while the shoes were made. Little did she know

that Gwydion and the boy had been plotting to get her down to their boat all along.

While Gwydion measured Aranrhod's feet, a bird flew over and landed on the deck of the ship. The boy took out a bow and arrow. He let an arrow fly. His shot hit the bird in the leg, which was considered to be the most difficult shot in archery. Aranrhod was very impressed.

"Truly," she said, "the lion aimed at it with a steady hand."[5]

Gwydion rejoiced. He took off his disguise and told Aranrhod that she had fulfilled her own prophecy. From that day forward, the boy would be called Lleu Llaw Gyffes, which means "Lion With the Steady Hand." Aranrhod was very angry at having been tricked. In her rage, she placed a new curse on Lleu. She swore he would never be allowed to carry weapons until she herself gave them to him.

Gwydion again determined to find a way around the curse. He brought Lleu home and trained him to be a warrior. When the boy was old enough to bear arms, they once again made a journey to Aranrhod's palace. This time, they disguised themselves as minstrels. Aranrhod greatly enjoyed songs and invited the pair in to sing for her and her household. She was so pleased with their performance that she fed them and even gave them shelter for the night.

Early in the morning, before anyone else was awake, Gwydion began another trick. He used all his magic powers to cast a spell. He made it seem as if the entire castle were surrounded by a fleet of enemy ships. Then he woke the household with cries of an attack.

Aranrhod sprang from bed. She was terrified when she saw all the ships and did not know what to do. She begged the minstrels for their help. Gwydion replied that they could fight, but that they lacked weapons. Aranrhod commanded her servants to provide weapons for Gwydion. Then she herself draped weapons over Lleu. By the time she was done, the illusion vanished. Gwydion began laughing and revealed his true identity.

Aranrhod realized that there had never been any ships. This time she was angrier than she had ever been before. She came up with her worst curse yet. She promised that Lleu would never have a human wife so long as he lived. Gwydion was not overly concerned—he had found his way around the other two curses; he would find a way around this one, too.

Gwydion thought the first step would be to go to Math, who was also a great magician. Together, they used their magic to create a woman from flower petals. They called her Blodeuwedd, which means "Flower Face." She was the most beautiful woman Lleu had ever seen. He immediately fell in love with her. He asked her to be his bride. She agreed and the happy couple were soon wed. As a gift, Gwydion presented them with a small castle near a lake.

The couple lived happily together. One day, though, Lleu left the palace to visit Math. While he was away, a stranger came hunting in the area. He was Gronw Pebyr, one of the gods of darkness. Blodeuwedd saw him in the woods and invited him into the palace. The two fell in love and began a secret affair. They decided to kill Lleu so they could be together. They plotted ways to murder him. Lleu, however, was invincible in battle and could be hurt in only one way. No one knew what this secret was. It was up to Blodeuwedd to find out her husband's one weakness.

When he returned from visiting Math, Blodeuwedd asked Lleu how he preserved his life. She lied and said she wanted to know in order to be able to protect against it

ever happening. Lleu replied that he could only be killed by a spear that had been worked on for one full year, but never crafted on Sundays or holidays. In addition, he would die only if the spear were thrown just after he had bathed, while he had one foot upon the bath and the other upon a goat's back. Blodeuwedd pretended to praise the heavens that his death was so unlikely.

Over the next year Blodeuwedd continued her secret affair. Gronw spent the time crafting the spear. When the full year had passed, Blodeuwedd asked Lleu to show her in detail how he could be killed. That way, she lied, she would know how to protect him if anything ever happened. The moment Lleu got into position, Gronw threw the spear. It had been dipped in poison. It sank deep into Lleu's flesh, but did not kill him. Instead, he turned into an eagle. The mighty bird let out a great cry and flew off. After he left, Gronw took over the palace and married Blodeuwedd.

News of what happened made its way to Gwydion. He set off to find his son. While searching, he ran into a servant, who mentioned to Gwydion that one of his master's pigs kept running off each day, but returned each night without fail. No one could figure out where it went during the day. Gwydion decided to follow the sow. It traveled a great distance, but finally stopped to graze beneath a tree. Gwydion looked to see what it was eating. He realized that the pig fed upon pieces of meat that were falling from the tree. It turned out that an eagle was at the top and the meat was the scraps from its kill. Gwydion felt in his heart that the eagle was his son.

Gwydion sang a song to the bird to coax it down. When it finally came down, Gwydion struck it with his wand. Lleu turned back into his human form. His father rejoiced, but

realized that his son was still very weak. Gwydion brought Lleu to Math to heal completely.

In the meantime, Gwydion went to track down the woman who had betrayed his son. Blodeuwedd heard he was coming and tried to run. Gwydion soon overtook her. When he caught her, he turned her into an owl. Blodeuwedd was forced to spend the rest of her life hunting at night in solitude, as an outcast from all other birds.

QUESTIONS AND ANSWERS

Q: *What unique curse plagued Math?*

A: Math could only live if his feet rested upon the lap of a virgin.

Q: *How did Gwydion and Lleu trick Aranrhod into coming to their boat?*

A: Gwydion and Lleu disguised themselves as leather craftsmen. They deliberately sized Aranrhod's shoes incorrectly so she would have to come to the boat herself to have her feet measured.

Q: *What is Lleu's full name and what does it mean?*

A: Lleu's full name is Lleu Llaw Gyffes. It means "lion with the steady hand."

Q: *What is the worst curse that Aranrhod lays upon her son?*

A: Aranrhod swears that Lleu will never marry a human woman so long as he lives.

Q: *How do Gwydion and Math make Lleu a wife?*

A: Gwydion and Math use their magic powers to make a woman out of flower petals. They call her Blodeuwedd, which means "Flower Face."

Q: *How does the pig help Gwydion find his son?*

A: The pig leads Gwydion to a tree, where an eagle is eating meat. The eagle turns out to be Lleu.

EXPERT COMMENTARY

As in the myths of any culture, the stories of the *Mabinogi* offer insight into the social codes and customs by which people were expected to abide. In terms of gender roles, for example, men are usually depicted as hunters, warriors, and landowners, while women are seen as symbols of fertility and the home. As scholar Roberta Valente illustrates, however, these traditional gender roles are actually reversed in the story of Gwydion and Aranrhod.

Aranrhod defies the norms by being a powerful, independent woman who possesses her own castle. Because she is unmarried, she is expected to be a virgin—but Aranrhod resists this code, as well. Valente writes:

> Presumably, Aranrhod would have known her true status, so her answer to Math takes on the quality of a lie, a denial of her sexual experience. A false claim of virginity before marriage was a legal violation, and though Math is not intending to marry Aranrhod, his dependence on the veracity [truth] of her claim is as urgent as that of any bridegroom.[6]

In addition, Aranrhod rejects the traditional role of motherhood by cursing her own son.

Gwydion becomes the nurturer in her place, despite the fact that he is a man. According to Valente, Gwydion takes on "the female power of creation one more time to 'give birth' to Blodeuwedd."[7] Of course, this gender role switching fails Gwydion, just as it fails Aranrhod for lying about her virginity. In a way, he is punished for his actions when the woman he has created betrays both him and his son.

6

PWYLL, HEAD OF HADES

INTRODUCTION

The British Celts were more susceptible to the invasions of the Romans, and later of the Anglo-Saxons than their Irish counterparts. In fact, some historians argue that British Celts migrated to Ireland during the invasions to escape the foreign conquest.[1] The stories from the Welsh tradition were also recorded later than those of the Irish vein. As a result, the versions of Welsh stories that still exist today tend to reflect greater outside influence.

On the European continent, for example, medieval tales of the eleventh and twelfth centuries focused on the adventures of great knights and their quests. This genre of literature was known generally as the romance. The Continental romances depicted the strict codes of conduct these knights lived by and the importance of courtesy at their courts. For example, a chivalrous knight was never expected to kill a wounded enemy. To do so would be dishonorable. In the following story of how Pwyll became lord of the underworld, some of the Celtic versions of these codes are revealed.

PWYLL, HEAD OF HADES

Pwyll was ruler of Dyfed, located in the southwest corner of what is now Wales. One day, Pwyll left his capital with a group of his men to go hunting in a far-off region called Glynn Cuch. Pwyll blew his horn and released his hounds to begin the hunt. In a short time, he got separated from his companions.

The lord followed the sound of his hounds. As he did so, he heard another pack of hounds, not his own, advancing toward him. At a clearing in the forest, Pwyll saw his hounds chasing the other pack, who were in turn running after a mighty stag. The strange hounds overtook the stag and brought it to the ground.

As he took a closer look at the hounds, Pwyll noticed that they were like none he had ever seen before. They were dazzling white with brilliant red ears. These hounds came from the underworld, although Pwyll did not know it at the time.[2] As he approached, he drove the red-eared hounds away from the stag. Pwyll saw no other human being nearby, so he decided to claim the killed stag as his own.

While Pwyll was tending to the stag, a stranger rode up on a great gray horse. The stranger told Pwyll that he had

never met a more dishonorable person. "In no man," said the stranger, "have I seen greater discourtesy than driving away the pack which has killed a stag and baiting one's own pack upon it."[3]

Pwyll apologized sincerely for his mistake. He offered to do anything the stranger asked to make up for his fault. The man on the gray horse was Arawn, a king of Annwn, the underworld. Arawn explained that a rival king of the underworld, Hafgan, was constantly raging war on him. The only way for Pwyll to make up for his sin was to defeat Hafgan in a battle, which was scheduled to take place a year and a day from then.

Pwyll agreed to take on Hafgan, but asked how he would do it. Arawn cast a spell that switched the two men's likenesses. Pwyll would go to the underworld and rule in Arawn's place, while Arawn would return to Dyfed. No one would be able to tell the difference. After Pwyll had defeated Hafgan, the two men would return to their own shapes and lives.

Just as Arawn had said, no one in Annwn suspected Pwyll was anyone other than their king. As he returned from his hunt, he was greeted with a great feast. He dined on the best food and wine that he had ever had. At the feast, Pwyll sat next to Arawn's wife, who was the most beautiful woman he had ever seen.

That night, the queen led Pwyll to bed. Pwyll, however, would not say a word to her. He slept with his back to her and would not touch her at all. For every day over the next year, they spent their time talking, dining, and celebrating. But every night, no matter how affectionate they were during the day, Pwyll would not lay a hand on the queen.

At last the day came when Pwyll was to fight Hafgan. With one blow, Pwyll shattered Hafgan's armor and shield, killing him almost instantly. Hafgan's men pledged their allegiance to the victor. In Arawn's place, Pwyll had managed to double the size of the kingdom.

The next day, Pwyll and Arawn met at Glynn Cuch. They restored their shapes and returned to their rightful lands.

Arawn was happy to return to his home and his people. Of course, they knew nothing of his absence. He spent the day dining and celebrating, just as Pwyll had done in his place. That night, as he got into bed with his wife, he spoke softly to her and held her lovingly in his arms. The queen stopped Arawn. She asked why he was caressing her all of a sudden after ignoring her for a full year. Arawn realized

what a good friend he had found in Pwyll. He told his wife the truth about what had happened over the last year. She agreed that Pwyll was an uncommonly chivalrous man not to take advantage of another man's wife.

Meanwhile, in Dyfed, Pwyll asked his nobles how the past year had compared to previous ones. The men replied that it had been a particularly wonderful year. Pwyll admitted that he could not accept the credit. He let his people know of the switch. They all exclaimed how lucky Pwyll was to have found such a good friend.

Pwyll and Arawn continued to be good friends for life. Each sent the other horses, hounds, or whatever other

treasures he thought his friend would enjoy. And because Pwyll had ruled Annwn and expanded its boundaries, Arawn even granted him the title Head of the Underworld.

Even with his new title, Pwyll continued to rule in Dyfed. Outside his palace was a hill said to have magical properties. One of Pwyll's men told him that when a man of royal blood sits upon it, he is either struck down by mighty blows, or he beholds a wonder. Pwyll did not think he would be struck down and he wanted very much to see a wonder, so he sat on the mound.

As Pwyll sat there, a beautiful woman dressed in dazzling gold appeared riding on horseback. Anyone who looked at her would have said she was riding at a very slow pace. But when Pwyll sent a man on foot to find out her name, he could not catch her. Soon, she disappeared over the horizon.

The next day, Pwyll sat on the mound again. This time, he had his man ready on horseback to ride after her. But again, once she appeared, he was unable to catch her although she appeared to move slowly. On the third day, Pwyll decided to overtake her himself. He sat on the hill and waited for the mysterious woman to arrive. As she rode by, Pwyll mounted his horse. Ride as he might, he was unable to catch her. He pushed his horse as fast as it could go, but still could not overtake the woman.

In desperation, Pwyll called out to the woman to stop. "I will, gladly," she said, "and it would have been better for your horse had you asked me that earlier."[4] She told Pwyll that her name was Rhiannon, daughter of Heveydd the Old. Rhiannon had been promised in marriage to a man she did not love. She had come to find Pwyll to help her, because he was the man of her dreams. Pwyll was very happy to hear this because he, too, was falling in love. The

pair worked out a plan whereby they would meet a year and day from then at Heveydd's court.

On the appointed date, Pwyll and ninety-nine of his companions arrived at the old man's court. As Rhiannon had promised, a great feast was waiting for Pwyll and his men. Everyone sat down together to dine. Pwyll sat between Rhiannon and her father.

As they were eating, a tall young man approached. He asked Pwyll for a favor. Pwyll promised to grant whatever the young man might ask. Rhiannon looked terrified of this response. She knew that by the rules of chivalry, a man must never go back on a favor he has agreed to. Rhiannon's instinct proved correct when the young man asked for her hand in marriage. He was none other than Gwawl, the man she had been promised to, but did not want to wed.

Pwyll apologized to Rhiannon, telling her that he had not known who the man was. Rhiannon replied that he had no choice but to honor himself and thus grant Gwawl his favor. Pwyll refused, saying he could never part from her. Rhiannon told him to do as he must, but that she would find a way to prevent the marriage from ever taking place. Pwyll trusted her and told Gwawl to return in one year's time. At that date, Pwyll would have a great feast prepared and would grant Gwawl Rhiannon's hand in marriage.

The next year, the feast was made ready. Rhiannon sat next to her unwanted suitor. Pwyll waited outside with ninety-nine men. While the men stood outside, Pwyll entered the feast, disguised as an old beggar. He held in his hand a magic bag that Rhiannon had given him a year earlier. No matter how much was put in the bag, it would never be filled.

Just as Gwawl had a year earlier, Pwyll requested a

favor. He told Gwawl that he was but a poor beggar and asked that his little bag be filled with food. Gwawl agreed and ordered his men to fill the bag with meat. They brought serving after serving, but the bag remained nearly empty. Finally, Gwawl asked Pwyll if it would ever be filled. Pwyll responded that it would not be filled unless a nobleman of rich possessions pressed the food down with both his feet.

Gwawl agreed and stepped into the bag. As soon as both feet were inside, Pwyll tipped the sack over and tied it shut. Then he blew on his horn as a signal for his men to attack the court. As each man entered the court, he hit the sack with a stick and asked "What is this?" "A badger" was always the reply. This was the first playing of a game called "Badger in the Bag," a less brutal version of which continues to be played by British children.

Rhiannon and her father asked Pwyll to stop beating Gwawl. They suggested Pwyll release him on the condition that he would offer gifts and promise never to seek vengeance. Gwawl gladly agreed. He departed for his own country to heal the many bruises he had received while in the bag.

Once Gwawl had left, the hall was once more made ready for a wedding. This time, of course, the couple to be wed was Pwyll and Rhiannon. They feasted and celebrated all night. When the wedding was over, the couple returned to Dyfed to rule the country.

QUESTIONS AND ANSWERS

Q: *What was different about the hounds Pwyll saw while hunting?*

A: The hounds Pwyll saw were dazzling white with bright red ears. They were hounds from the underworld.

Q: *Why did Arawn call Pwyll the most dishonorable man he had ever known?*

A: Arawn called Pwyll dishonorable because Pwyll had claimed a stag as his own even though he did not kill it himself.

Q: *What was said to happen when a man of noble birth sat upon the mound outside Pwyll's palace?*

A: When a man of noble birth sat on the mound he was either struck down by blows or he saw a wonder.

Q: *How did Pwyll finally get Rhiannon to stop riding her horse?*

A: Rhiannon stopped riding once Pwyll asked her to.

Q: *What favor did Gwawl ask of Pwyll at the feast?*

A: Gwawl asked for Rhiannon's hand in marriage. Pwyll had no choice but to agree or else he would lose his honor.

Q: *What magic powers did the bag that Rhiannon gave Pwyll possess?*

A: The bag never filled up, no matter how much was placed inside it.

EXPERT COMMENTARY

The importance of chivalry is highlighted again and again in the story of Pwyll. To make up for his error, Pwyll agrees without hesitation to take over the underworld in Arawn's place. Once there, he refuses to dishonor the Queen by sleeping with her. He holds to a promise he has made, even if it means another man might marry the woman he loves. There is no debate that chivalry is an important theme in the myth. The question, however, is for whom these morals were intended.

Celtic scholar Catherine McKenna argues that the main audience for the myth was aristocracy.

> Socially, of course, the original audience of the Four Branches may be taken to have been an aristocratic one. This is attested by the preoccupation of the tales with the activities of kings and lords, as well as by what is known about the circumstances in which literature was produced in medieval Celtic and in early European society generally.[5]

In addition, there are many descriptions of hunting and feasting, which were "the major peacetime activities of aristocratic life."[6]

If the story of Pwyll was told primarily at aristocratic courts, then the lord of the underworld would have served as an example for the young lords and princes who were listening. As McKenna points out:

> In this model of lordship he [a prince] would have seen heroism, justice, and promotion of the land's fertility and prosperity—three qualities associated throughout Celtic tradition with effective sovereignty.[7]

7

CULHWCH AND OLWEN

INTRODUCTION

Perhaps the best-known legacy that Celtic mythology has left the world is the body of literature surrounding the great King Arthur. Stories of Arthur and his famous knights have fascinated audiences for centuries. The sagas have served as the inspiration for countless poems, books, plays, and even movies.

The Arthurian legends with which most people are familiar, however, bear little resemblance to the original Welsh myths. The Celtic Arthurian stories are generally considered to have originated around 1000 A.D., although they were not first recorded until the eleventh century. The basis for the Welsh myths was a real-life sixth century chieftain who fought against the Anglo-Saxon invasion. These myths were first recorded in the *Mabinogi*, among other sources.

The story of Arthur first became known to people outside the Celtic world through the work of a twelfth-century writer named Geoffrey of Monmouth. His work was written in Latin and titled *Historia Regum Britanniae*, meaning "History of British Kings." In France, Chrétien de Troyes penned his own Arthurian legends in the twelfth century. He added to the myths the love affair between Guinevere and Lancelot and the quest for the Holy Grail. Neither of these elements existed in the original. Even in thirteenth-century Germany, poets were incorporating their own elements into the story.[1] Eventually, the myths took on a life of their own—one that was far removed from the original Celtic myths.

The first full-fledged Arthurian tale within the Celtic tradition is considered to be the following story of Culhwch and Olwen. In it, Arthur plays a very different role than that

which readers typically associate with him. He is not only a ruler, but also a participant in the quests. His wife, in Welsh called Gwenhwyfar, does not even appear in this particular story. Likewise, with the exception of Kai (or Kay in English) most of the knights are different than those people have come to associate with the legends.

CULHWCH AND OLWEN

Culhwch was the son of Cilydid and Goleuddydd and the
cousin of the famous King Arthur. When Goleuddydd died,
Cilydid took another wife. The new wife thought Culhwch
would make a good husband for her own daughter. When
Culhwch refused her request, she became very angry. She
laid a curse on him that the only woman he could ever
marry was Olwen, daughter of the fearsome giant
Yspaddaden Pencawr. Yspaddaden would not allow any
man to marry his daughter because an ancient curse
promised he would die on the wedding day.

Even so, Culhwch blushed at the sound of Olwen's
name. He fell in love with the very idea of her and went to
his father to ask how he could win her. Cilydid reminded
his son that he was King Arthur's cousin. He suggested he
go to Arthur's court and ask for Olwen as a favor.

After a long journey, Culhwch arrived at the gates of
Arthur's palace. It was late and the gates had been closed
for the night. The gatekeeper explained that it was Arthur's
custom to keep the gates locked until morning. Culhwch
flatly refused this response. He demanded to be allowed
in. He swore that if he were not, he would let out a shriek

so loud and so shrill that it would cause every pregnant woman in the land to miscarry her child. The gatekeeper brought this news to Arthur. Although several of his knights advised him against doing so, Arthur went against custom and allowed Culhwch to enter.

After greeting each other, Arthur offered his cousin food and drink. Culhwch explained that he was there for a much greater purpose and that he had a favor to ask. Arthur promised to grant him whatever he asked. Hearing this Culhwch replied, "Then I ask for Olwen daughter of Chief Giant Ysbaddaden, and I invoke her in the name of your warriors."[2]

Neither Arthur nor any of his knights had heard of Olwen, but they promised to help Culhwch find her nonetheless. Arthur ordered his most skilled warriors to accompany Culhwch on his journey. Among the men who went along were Kai, who could hold his breath for nine days and go without sleep for nine nights. With Kai came his constant companion Bedwyr, who was as fast with a sword as he was beautiful. The party was rounded out by Gwrhyr, who could speak the language of any man or animal, Gwalchmei, who could leave no adventure unachieved, and Menw, who could make himself and his companions invisible.

The party traveled together until they saw a huge fortress on an open plain. Feeding on the plain was a seemingly endless number of sheep. They were watched over by a hulking shepherd and his huge dog. Menw put a spell on the dog so that they could approach the shepherd without harm. The party asked the shepherd his name and whose fortress it was. He replied that he was Custennin. The fortress belonged to Yspaddaden, who Custennin and his wife hated. The evil giant had killed all but one of their twenty-four sons. They kept the only survivor hidden in a

stone chest to keep him from harm. Kai offered to take the boy under his wing and train him as a knight. In return for his generous offer, Custennin's wife offered to secure a secret meeting between Olwen and Culhwch.

Messengers were dispatched and Olwen came down to the plain to wash her hair. According to the poets of old:

> Her hair was yellower than broom, her skin whiter than sea-foam. . . . Neither the eye of a mewed hawk nor the eye of a thrice-mewed falcon was fairer than hers; her [skin was] whiter than the breast of a white swan, her cheeks were redder than the reddest foxgloves, and anyone who saw her would fall deeply in love.[3]

Culhwch and Olwen talked together at Custennin's home and quickly fell in love. As Olwen stood up to return home, she told Culhwch to ask her father for her hand in marriage and not to deny anything he might ask of him. In return, she promised to spend the rest of her days with him.

The next day, the party made for Yspaddaden's castle. They killed the nine gatekeepers and made their way straight to the giant's chambers. Culhwch announced his intention to marry Olwen. The giant glared at them. He said he would think about the request and give them an answer the next day. As they turned to go, he grabbed a poisoned spear and threw it at them. But Bedwyr, quick as lightning, caught it and hurled it back, wounding the giant's knee.

The next day the same thing happened. Yspaddaden told them to return and threw a second spear as they left. Menw caught the spear and this time pierced the giant's chest. The third day they repeated the ritual once more. This time, Culhwch caught the spear and threw it back so hard that it went through Yspaddaden's eye and came out

the other side. The giant finally agreed to sit down with Culhwch and his party to discuss his daughter's marriage.

Yspaddaden agreed to let Culhwch marry Olwen, but only after he completed several tasks. The giant then listed thirty-nine tasks, each more impossible then the last. For example, Culhwch was to plow a vast hill in one day's time, which could only be achieved if they captured two magic oxen to lead the plow, which could only be driven by a certain plowman, and so on. After Yspaddaden named each feat to be completed or item to be brought back, Culhwch simply responded, "It will be easy for me to get that, though you think otherwise."[4]

Culhwch and his party made their way back to Arthur's court. On the way, Kai fulfilled one of the trials by tricking a giant named Gwrnach into giving him his sword. When they arrived at court, they explained to the king what they must do. Arthur immediately promised his help and resources. The group set out to accomplish their tasks. They realized that the most dangerous one would be obtaining the comb and shears that rested between the ears of Twrch Trwyth, a king transformed into a monstrous boar.

On their way to find the boar king, Arthur and his companions attempted to fulfill another of their tasks—to find Mabon, the son of Modron who had been kidnapped when he was only three days old. Arthur instructed Gwyhyr to ask an ancient Blackbird if he knew of Mabon's whereabouts. The Blackbird answered that while he had been sitting in that spot long enough to peck an anvil to the size of a nut, he had never heard anyone speak of the boy. The bird suggested they ask a beast older than he, the Stag of Rhedenvre. The Stag could not help them, nor could an old Owl nor an ancient Eagle. Finally, though, they were directed toward the Salmon of Lake Llyw, who was said to

have been the oldest living creature in the world. The Salmon indeed knew where Mabon lived. He even offered to take Kai and Gwrhyr there on his shoulders. Together they made their way to a stone house, where they heard terrible wailing. It was Mabon, begging for his freedom. Kai and Gwyhyr released Mabon, who then helped them fulfill many of their other tasks.

After much time, Arthur decided he and his men were ready to take on Twrch. They advanced to the castle where the boar king lived with his seven young pig sons. The companions fought Twrch for three days with little results.

Finally, Arthur sent Gwrhyr in the shape of a bird to speak with Twrch. Gwrhyr begged the boar king to give up his comb and scissors in order to put an end to all the fighting. Twrch not only refused, he promised to do even more damage to the land and Arthur's men.

Enraged, Twrch and his pigs swam across the sea into Wales. Arthur and his men followed. They made their way all over Britain chasing Twrch, encountering many adventures and even fulfilling other tasks in the process. Over a long period of time, the pig sons were killed one by one until Twrch alone remained. Finally, they cornered the king and were able to grab the comb and scissors—but not without great effort and cost on their part. Twrch managed to escape before Arthur had a chance to kill him.

With the comb in hand, Arthur had succeeded in helping Culhwch fulfill his trials as promised. They made their way back to Yspaddaden, bringing him every treasure he had required. The gifts he had demanded turned out to be his death wish. When Culhwch asked if Olwen was his, Yspaddaden replied, "She is. And you need not thank me, rather Arthur, who won her for you; of my own will you would have never got her. Now it is time for you to kill me."[5]

With that, one of Arthur's men grabbed the giant and beheaded him. Yspaddaden's head was placed on a pole on the wall. Arthur seized the fortress and all the treasures. Culhwch, of course, took Olwen and the couple was soon married.

QUESTIONS AND ANSWERS

Q: *How is Culhwch related to King Arthur?*

A: Culhwch is Arthur's cousin.

Q: *What custom did Culhwch break when he first arrived at Arthur's court?*

A: Culhwch insisted on being shown into the castle even though it was after dark and the gates had already been locked.

Q: *What special skills did Kai possess?*

A: Kai could hold his breath for nine days and go without sleep for nine nights.

Q: *Why did Custennin the shepherd hate Yspaddaden?*

A: Custennin hated Yspaddaden because the giant killed all but one of his twenty-four sons. The one surviving child was hidden in a box for safekeeping.

Q: *What did Arthur and his men believe would be the most difficult task to fulfill?*

A: Arthur and his men believed it would be most difficult to obtain the comb and scissors that rested between the ears of Twrch, the boar king.

Q: *How long had the Blackbird that Gwrhyr spoke to been sitting in the same place?*

A: The Blackbird had been sitting in the same place long enough to peck an anvil down to the size of a nut.

EXPERT COMMENTARY

French poet Chrétien de Troyes wrote his own version of the Arthurian saga approximately eighty years after the Welsh tales were first published.[6] Scholar Armel Diverres notes the many differences between the two stories. To begin with, while there are examples of chivalry in the Welsh tales, it is not stressed to nearly the same degree as in the French. In fact, Diverres argues that:

> the one touch of courtliness in Arthur's personal conduct is to be found in the manner in which he overrides [Kai's] objections to Culhwch's entry into his hall until the meal is over, on the grounds that it would go against court protocol.[7]

Rather than denying Culhwch's rather rude demand or chastising him for his behavior, Arthur graciously invites him in and even grants him a favor.

In addition, unlike in the French tales, the Welsh Arthur is a more active member of the adventures. As Diverres writes:

> In the Welsh tale the quests are undertaken by members of his [Arthur's] warband, forming a group, not by a single warrior, while the king participates in a number of them and plays the leading role in a few, particularly the hunt for Twrch Twyth.[8]

In the Chrétien de Troyes version, however, Arthur only "preside[s] over a court in which chivalry and refinement are predominant . . . there is no glorification of Arthur's own martial pursuits, merely those of his knights."[9]

 GLOSSARY

Anglo-Saxons—A Germanic people who invaded and ruled England from the fifth century A.D. to the time of the Norman Conquest in 1066.

Celts—One of the great founding civilizations of Europe. At various times from the second millennium B.C. on, the Celts occupied areas of Europe as far-ranging as the British Isles to northern Spain to as far east as Transylvania. The Celts were eventually conquered by the Romans, Anglo-Saxons, and Normans. In terms of language, the Celts survive in the modern speakers of Ireland, Highland Scotland, the Isle of Man, Cornwall, Wales, and Brittany.

Cymric—Relating to the language of the Celts in Wales, Brittany, and Cornwall.

druid—A member of the learned class among the ancient Celts. Druids served as religious leaders, magicians, poets, advisors, lawyers, and more in Celtic culture.

Eriu—one of the ancient names for the island of Ireland. The Anglicized version is Erin. Eriu was also one of the wives of the three kings of Ireland during the time of the Milesian Invasion.

Fianna—The followers of Finn Mac Cool. The Fianna were a band of warriors whose adventures make up the Fennian cycle of Celtic mythology.

Gaelic—Relating to the language of the Celts in Ireland, the Isle of Man, and the Scottish Highlands.

Mabinogi—A collection of Welsh tales based on mythology, folklore, and heroic legends. *The Mabinogion* was first transcribed between 1300 and 1425, although the tales themselves are believed to have originated much earlier.

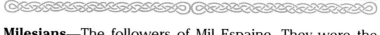

Milesians—The followers of Mil Espaine. They were the first human invaders of Ireland.

Ossian—A collection of poems by Scotsman James Macpherson that tells the story of Oisín. The authenticity of Macpherson's translations were a subject of great debate among literary circles of the nineteenth century.

pagan—Referring to a polytheistic religion, or a religion that worships multiple gods. Pagan religions are often close to nature, worshiping the natural forces of the universe, such as the sky, the water, the sun, fertility, and death.

síd—A mound or hill that served as the secret dwelling place of the Tuatha Dé Danaan after the Milesian Invasion.

Tuatha Dé Danaan—The children of the Mother Goddess Danu. The Tuatha Dé Danaan were the first inhabitants and invaders of Ireland of any great significance in Celtic mythology. The Welsh counterparts to these gods are the children of Dôn.

Ulster—The northernmost province of ancient Ireland. Ulster still exists in Ireland today and comprises part of what is known as Northern Ireland.

CHAPTER NOTES

Preface

1. Peter Berresford Ellis, *The Dictionary of Celtic Mythology* (London: Constable and Company, 1992), p. 1.

2. Simon James, "The Conventional History of the Celts," *Ancient Celts Page* <www.ares.u-net.com/convent.htm> (June 24, 2002).

3. Ellis, p. 2.

4. Tim Bond, "The Development of Christian Society in Early England," *Britannia: The Church: Past and Present* <www.britannia.com/church/bond1.html> (June 24, 2002).

5. Charles Squire, *Celtic Myth and Legend: From Arthur and the Round Table to the Gaelic Gods and the Giants They Battled—The Celebrated Comprehensive Treasury of Celtic Mythology, Legend, and Poetry* (Franklin Lakes, NJ: New Page Books, 2001), p. 36.

6. Bond, <www.britannia.com/church/bond1.html>.

7. Ibid.

8. Ellis, p. 4.

Chapter 1. The Coming of the Tuatha Dé Danaan

1. Charles Squire, *Celtic Myth and Legend: From Arthur and the Round Table to the Gaelic Gods and the Giants They Battled—The Celebrated Comprehensive Treasury of Celtic Mythology, Legend, and Poetry* (Franklin Lakes, NJ: New Page Books, 2001), p. 65.

2. T. W. Rolleston, *Myths and Legends of the Celtic Race* (New York: Schocken Books, 1986), p. 105.

3. Ibid., pp. 107–108.

4. Squire, p. 84.

5. Ibid., p. 85.

6. Ibid.

7. Alexei Kondratiev, "Lugus: The Many-Gifted Lord," <http://imbas.org/lugus.htm> (June 24, 2002).

8. Rolleston, pp. 137–138.

Chapter 2. The Milesian Invasion

1. Charles Squire, *Celtic Myth and Legend: From Arthur and the Round Table to the Gaelic Gods and the Giants They Battled—*

The Celebrated Comprehensive Treasury of Celtic Mythology, Legend, and Poetry (Franklin Lakes, NJ: New Page Books, 2001), p. 122.

2. Peter Berresford Ellis, *The Dictionary of Celtic Mythology* (London: Constable and Company, 1992), p. 23.

3. Ibid., p. 84.

4. Ibid.

Chapter 3. Cúchulainn and Emer

1. Peter Berresford Ellis, *Dictionary of Celtic Mythology* (London: Constable and Company, 1992), p. 185.

2. Eleanor Hull, *The Cuchullin Saga in Irish Literature* (New York: AMS Press, 1972), p. 10.

3. Charles Squire, *Celtic Myth and Legend, Revised Edition* (Franklin Lakes, NJ: New Page Books, 2001), p. 162.

4. Ibid., p. 162.

5. Claire Booss, ed., *A Treasury of Irish Myth, Legend*, and Folklore (New York: Gramercy Books, 1986), p. 380.

6. T. W. Rolleston, *Myths and Legends of the Celtic Race* (New York: Schocken Books, 1986), p. 188.

7. Ellis, p. 102.

8. Booss, p. 381.

9. Thomas Kinsella, *The Tain: Translated from the Irish Epic Tain Bo Cuailnge* (London: Oxford University Press, 1970), p. 34.

10. Booss, p. 385.

11. Rolleston, p. 195.

12. Kinsella, p. 38.

13. Ibid., p. xiii.

14. Rolleston, p. 187, n.1.

15. Squire, p. 155.

Chapter 4. Oisín

1. Charles Squire, *Celtic Myth and Legend*, Revised Edition (Franklin Lakes, NJ: New Page Books, 2001), p. 223.

2. Peter Berresford Ellis, *Dictionary of Celtic Mythology* (London: Constable and Company, 1992), p. 154.

3. Paul J. deGategno, *James Macpherson* (Boston: Twayne Publishers, 1989), p. 1.

4. Ibid., p. 123.

Chapter 5. Gwydion and Aranrhod

1. Peter Berresford Ellis, *Dictionary of Celtic Mythology* (London: Constable and Company, 1992), p. 221.

2. Ibid., p. 149.

3. Ibid., p. 87.

4. Charles Squire, *Celtic Myth and Legend*, Revised Edition (Franklin Lakes, NJ: New Page Books, 2001), p. 263.

5. Ibid.

6. Roberta L. Valente, "Gwydion and Aranrhod: Crossing the Borders of Gender in Math," *The Mabinogi: A Book of Essays*, C. W. Sullivan, ed. (New York: Garland Publishing, 1996), p. 338.

7. Ibid., p. 342.

Chapter 6. Pwyll, Head of Hades

1. Peter Berresford Ellis, *Dictionary of Celtic Mythology* (London: Constable and Company, 1992), p. 49.

2. Charles Squire, *Celtic Myth and Legend*, Revised Edition (Franklin Lakes, NJ: New Page Books, 2001), p. 280.

3. *The Mabinogion*, Jeffrey Gantz, trans. (New York: Penguin, 1976), p. 47.

4. Ibid., p. 54.

5. Catherine McKenna, "The Theme of Sovereignty in Pwyll" *In The Mabinogi: A Book of Essays*, C. W. Sullivan, ed. (New York: Garland, 1996), p. 309.

6. Ibid., p. 310.

7. Ibid., p. 316.

Chapter 7. Culhwch and Olwen

1. Peter Berresford Ellis, *Dictionary of Celtic Mythology* (London: Constable and Company, 1992), pp. 32–34.

2. *The Mabinogion*, Jeffrey Gantz, trans. (New York: Penguin, 1976), p. 140.

3. Ibid., pp. 151, 152.

4. Ibid., p. 155.

5. Ibid., pp. 175–176.

6. Armel Diverres, "Arthur in *Culhwch and Olwen* and in the Romances of Chrétien de Troyes," *Culture and the King: The Social Implications of the Arthurian Legend*, Martin B. Shichtman and James P. Carley, ed. (Albany, NY: SUNY Press, 1994), p. 54.

7. Ibid., p. 57.

8. Ibid., p. 64.

9. Ibid.

FURTHER READING

BOOKS

Brassey, Richard and Stewart Ross. *Story of Ireland.* London: Orion, 2001.

Haywood, John and Barry Cunliffe. *Atlas of the Celtic World.* London: Thames & Hudson, 2001.

Hestler, Anna. *Wales.* New York: Benchmark Books, 2001.

James, Simon. *Exploring the World of the Celts.* London: Thames & Hudson, 1993.

Lassieur, Allison. *The Celts.* San Diego: Lucent, 2001.

Martell, Hazel Mary. *Myths and Civilization of the Celts.* New York: Peter Bedrick Books, 1999.

Rees, Rosemary. *The Ancient Romans.* Portsmouth, N.H.: Heineman Library, 1999.

INTERNET ADDRESSES

Celtic Mythology
  <http://www.pantheon.org/areas/mythology/europe/celtic/articles.html>

The Mabinogion
  <http://www.cyberphile.co.uk/~taff/taffnet/mabinogion/mabinogion.htm>

INDEX